Editor
Barbara Wally, M.S.

Editorial Project Manager
Ina Massler Levin, M.A.

Editor in Chief
Sharon Coan, M.S. Ed.

Illustrator
Howard Chaney

Cover Artist
Sue Fullam

Art Coordinator
Cheri Macoubrie Wilson

Creative Director
Elayne Roberts

Imaging
Ralph Olmedo, Jr.

Product Manager
Phil Garcia

Publishers
Rachelle Cracchiolo, M.S. Ed.
Mary Dupuy Smith, M.S. Ed.

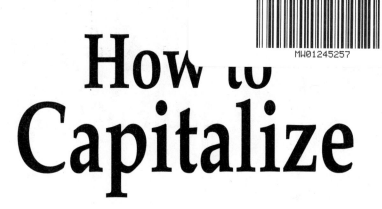

How to Capitalize

Grades 1–3

Author

J. L. Smith

Teacher Created Materials, Inc.
6421 Industry Way
Westminster, CA 92683
www.teachercreated.com

ISBN-1-57690-496-2

©1999 Teacher Created Materials, Inc.
Reprinted, 2000
Made in U.S.A.

Table of Contents

What It Is . . .

How to Capitalize is a resource for your classroom. You may use the book as a workbook to teach capitalization or use individual pages to supplement activities you are already doing in your classroom.

The Basics

Capitalization rules appropriate for students in grades 1–3 are presented in the book. Each page has a capitalization rule listed at the top. A brief description and examples of how to use the rule are listed for students to refer to during practice. Plenty of exercises are provided for students to practice the rule listed at the top of the page. Some concepts have only one page of practice. Other concepts have several pages of practice. It is up to the teacher to select which pages are appropriate for his or her class. A first-grade teacher may only use the first page or two of each section. A third-grade teacher may use the first page for review and select other pages for continued learning.

Assessment

Each section of the book is followed by several pages that can be used for assessment purposes. The assessments at the end of each section assess only the concepts covered in that section. The assessments at the end of the book cover many concepts covered throughout the book. Most assessments have two options. Again, they are provided for teacher choice. The first assessment is usually shorter and asks students to identify and correct capitalization errors on a line-by-line basis. The second assessment usually asks the student to copy a paragraph, correcting any capitalization errors. A student self-assessment is provided at the end of the book for students to reflect on the things learned throughout the unit.

Additional Resources

In addition, a handy capitalization reference sheet is provided for you on page 44. This sheet can be copied and distributed for each student in the class to keep in his or her notebook or the teacher can use it as a personal reference. Posters which list the capitalization rules covered in this book are provided on pages 45–46. Again, these posters can be distributed to students as references or can be enlarged and displayed on the wall as a reminder of capitalization rules. The resources section concludes with an answer key for each of the practice exercises in the book.

Lowercase Letters, Capital Letters

Write the capital letter next to each lowercase letter.

aA   b   c   d

e   f   g   h

i   j   k   l

m   n   o   p

q   r   s   t

u   v   w   x

y   z

Missing Letters

Complete each blank by filling in the missing capital letter. The alphabet is listed below as a reference.

A B C D E F G H I J K L M N O P Q R S T U V W X Y Z

1. A   B   C   D   E   <u>F</u>   G   H   I

2. O   P   Q   R   ___   T   U   V   W

3. S   T   ___   V   W   X   Y   Z

4. F   G   H   I   J   ___   L   M   N   O

5. C   D   E   ___   G   H   I   J   K   ___

6. N   ___   P   Q   R   S   T   U   ___   W

7. G   ___   I   J   K   ___   M   N   O

8. V   ___   X   Y   ___

9. Q   R   ___   T   ___   V   ___   X

10. J   ___   ___   M   ___   O   ___   ___   R   ___   T

Capital Art

Capital letters can be used as the basis for drawings. The letters B and P can be made into animals. Can you guess what animals they are? Write your answers on the lines below.

_____   _____

Now it is your turn to try some capital art. What can you draw using the letters below?

J	**L**
D	**S**

Use the back of this paper to create some capital art on your own. Choose a capital letter (or two) from the alphabet and start drawing.

The Word *I*

Capitalization Rule: Capitalize the pronoun *I*.

The word *I* is always capitalized. Practice writing the word *I* on the lines below.

1. _____ lost my tooth.

2. _____ like to play on the swings.

3. _____ have six dollars.

4. _____ have a dog as a pet.

5. _____ read a good book.

6. Today _____ am going to the park.

7. _____ went to the library yesterday.

8. May _____ have a drink?

9. Tom and _____ played ball at recess.

10. _____ like to ride my bike.

I Am Important

Capitalization Rule: Capitalize the pronoun I.

Every time you write your name, you begin it with a capital letter. Often instead of saying your name, you use the word *I*. The word *I* is taking the place of a proper noun—your name. A word that replaces a noun is called a pronoun. Every time the word *I* is used in a sentence, it is capitalized. It does not matter whether the word is at the beginning, middle, or end of a sentence: *I* is always capitalized.

Rewrite the sentences below. Practice making the pronoun *I* a capital letter.

1. i like ice cream.

   _____

2. i have a pet lizard.

   _____

3. i am going to the park after school.

   _____

4. i helped my mom plant a garden.

   _____

5. On Sunday, i am going to my grandma's house.

   _____

6. i don't like spinach.

   _____

7. On Saturday, i am going to a birthday party.

   _____

8. i have a lot of homework today.

   _____

9. If i do my chores, i get an allowance.

   _____

10. i learned to ride a bike when i was six.

    _____

A Rainbow of Likes

Capitalization Rule: Capitalize the pronoun I.

Practice capitalizing the word *I* by completing the sentences in the rainbow. Write the capital letter *I* on the first blank of each sentence. Complete the sentence by telling what you like by filling in the second blank. When you are finished, color the rainbow lightly.

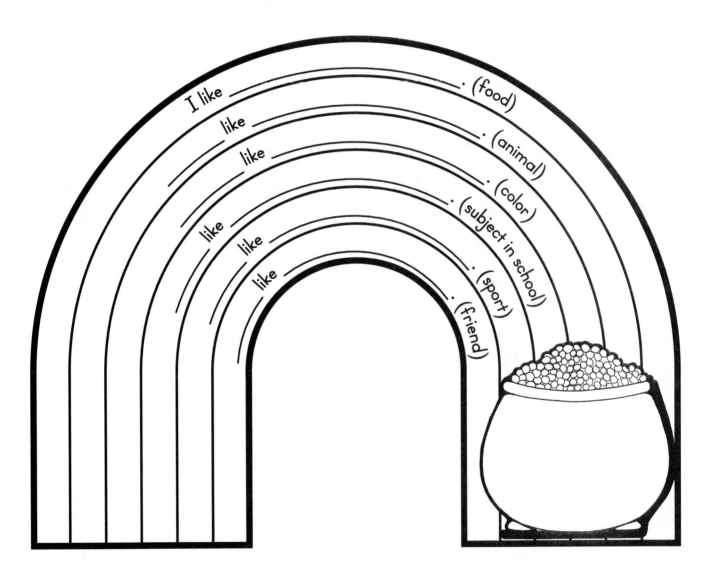

I like _____ . (food)

___ like _____ . (animal)

___ like _____ . (color)

___ like _____ . (subject in school)

___ like _____ . (sport)

___ like _____ . (friend)

All About Me

Capitalization Rule: Capitalize the pronoun I.

Answer the following questions in order to tell more about yourself. Begin each sentence using the word *I*. Be sure to capitalize the word *I*, and use a complete sentence. The first is started for you.

1. What is your name?

   I am _____

2. How old are you? _____

3. When were you born? _____

4. How many brothers do you have? _____

5. How many sisters do you have? _____

6. Do you have any pets? _____

7. What grade are you in? _____

8. What school do you go to? _____

Draw a picture of yourself.

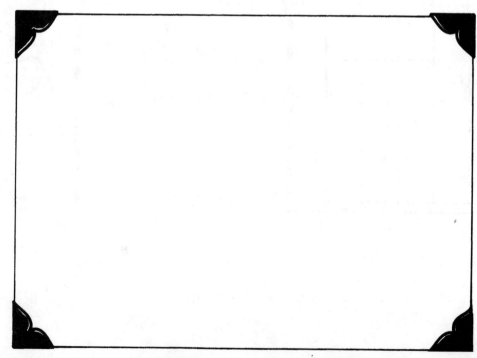

Start Right!

Capitalization Rule: Capitalize the first word in every sentence.

The first word in every sentence begins with a capital letter. The first word in each sentence below is written under the line. Practice capitalizing the first word in each sentence by writing it on the line.

1. _____ favorite color is yellow.
   my

2. _____ we play now?
   can

3. _____ you coming with us?
   are

4. _____ like to eat pizza.
   i

5. _____ are going to see a movie.
   we

6. _____ helped us make a cake.
   she

7. _____ are eggs in the nest.
   there

Get Off to a Good Start

Capitalization Rule: Capitalize the first word in every sentence.

The first word in every sentence begins with a capital letter. It is a way to show the reader that a new sentence has started.

Rewrite the following sentences. Begin the first word in the sentence with a capital letter.

1. today is my birthday.

   _____

2. my sister walked to the store with me.

   _____

3. we are going to play handball at recess.

   _____

4. can you come to the park with us?

   _____

5. our class has a pet lizard.

   _____

6. juan ate a sandwich for lunch.

   _____

7. the rabbit likes to eat carrots.

   _____

8. my blue crayon is missing.

   _____

9. dad is going to take us to the park this weekend.

   _____

10. i am going to the library after school.

   _____

Extension: On the back of this paper, write two sentences about what you like to do after school. Be sure to begin each sentence with a capital letter.

Picture Cues

Capitalization Rule: Capitalize the first word in every sentence.

Write a sentence about each of the pictures. Remember to capitalize the first word in the sentence.

1. _____

   _____

2. _____

   _____

3. _____

   _____

4. _____

   _____

5. _____

   _____

Fairy Tale Trivia

Capitalization Rule: Capitalize the first word in every sentence.

Test your knowledge of the fairy tale *Goldilocks and the Three Bears* while you practice capitalizing the first word in a sentence. Write a complete sentence to answer the questions below.

(**Note to teacher:** Be sure your students are familiar with the story *Goldilocks and the Three Bears* before having them answer these questions.)

1. What did the three bears do while their porridge cooled?

   _____

2. Who came into the three bears' house?

   _____

3. Why didn't Goldilocks eat Papa Bear's porridge?

   _____

4. Whose porridge did Goldilocks eat until it was gone?

   _____

5. What did Goldilocks do after she ate the porridge?

   _____

6. Why didn't Goldilocks like Mama Bear's chair?

   _____

7. Whose chair did Goldilocks break?

   _____

8. Which bear had a bed that was too hard?

   _____

9. What did Goldilocks do when she tried Baby Bear's bed?

   _____

10. What did Goldilocks do when she saw the bears?

   _____

Capitalization Assessment

Option 1

Show what you know about capitalization by rewriting the following sentences correctly.

1. my brother plays soccer.

   _____

2. dad gave me a doll.

   _____

3. i have to take out the trash.

   _____

4. we rode our bikes.

   _____

5. mom and i went to the store.

   _____

6. may I use your pencil?

   _____

7. i like to read books about bugs.

   _____

8. my favorite food is pizza.

   _____

Capitalization Assessment

Option 2

Rewrite the following paragraph, correcting the words that need capitalization. There are 12 words that need capital letters. Can you find all of them?

After School Fun

after school today, i went to my friend Sam's house. we played soccer. sam is good at scoring goals. i am good at passing the ball. after we played soccer, we went in the house. mrs. Matthews had cookies for us to eat. we had milk, too. milk is good with cookies. when we were done eating, we watched television. it started to get late, so i went home.

_____

_____

_____

_____

_____

_____

_____

_____

_____

_____

Being Specific

Capitalization Rule: Capitalize proper nouns.

All proper nouns begin with capital letters. Proper nouns are nouns which name specific persons, places, or things. For example, the word *Tuesday* names a specific day of the week. The word *Tuesday* is a proper noun and needs to be capitalized.

Circle the proper nouns in the sentences below. **Remember:** Proper nouns name specific persons, places, or things and always begin with capital letters.

1. On Tuesday, I am going to my grandma's house.

2. My birthday is in December.

3. I was born in Illinois.

4. We went boating on the Mississippi River.

5. My mom went to the grocery store with Anne.

6. If I don't feel better tomorrow, I will go see Dr. Andrews.

7. My favorite story is *The Little Engine That Could*.

8. Our whole family comes over on Thanksgiving Day.

9. My family went to Washington, D.C., this summer.

10. When I go to the library, I like to look at *Ranger Rick*.

Naming Things

Capitalization Rule: Capitalize proper nouns.

The name of a specific person, place, or thing needs to be capitalized. For example, my sister's name is Jane. The word *Jane* is capitalized because it names a specific person. Try some on your own. Think of a specific person, place, or thing that answers each question below. Be sure to capitalize each of them.

1. What is your name?_____

_____

2. In which month is your birthday? _____

_____

3. What day of the week is it? _____

_____

4. What is your brother's name? _____

_____

5. In what country do you live? _____

_____

6. What is your sister's name?_____

_____

7. On what street do you live? _____

_____

8. What is your favorite restaurant?_____

_____

9. In what state do you live? _____

_____

10. What is your favorite holiday? _____

_____

Name It

Capitalization Rule: Capitalize proper nouns.

Proper nouns that name specific persons are capitalized. Your name is a proper noun. When you write your name, you capitalize the first letter. If your name is Neil, you capitalize the *N* in *Neil*. Not only do you need to capitalize your first name, you also need to capitalize your last name. Your middle name is capitalized, too. Any word that names a specific person begins with a capital letter.

Practice capitalizing the names of people by writing these names on the lines. Be sure to capitalize first, middle, and last names.

1.   roger taper   _____

2.   silvia mantos   _____

3.   clarissa choi   _____

4.   tammy lynn witter   _____

5.   victor jason lee   _____

The name of your pet would be capitalized too. Write down the names of pets that you have. If you do not have a pet, write down the names of pets that you know.

_____

_____

_____

The pets below do not have names. Think of a name for each pet. Write the name on the line provided. Remember to capitalize the name of the pet.

_____   _____   _____   _____

Unique People

Capitalization Rule: Capitalize proper nouns. Capitalize the names of people.

The names of people are proper nouns and need to be capitalized. Try to fill in all of the boxes below by finding someone to fit each description. Practice capitalizing names by writing the name of the person in the box.

_____ was born in another state.	_____ wears glasses.
_____ has a birthday in May.	_____ loves to read.
_____ has brown eyes.	_____ likes pickles.
_____ has long hair.	_____ knows how to ride a bike.
_____ has more than one brother.	_____ went to preschool.
_____ wears a backpack to school.	_____ plays on a sports team.

Extension: Choose five names from the boxes above. On the back of this paper, write a complete sentence about each person.

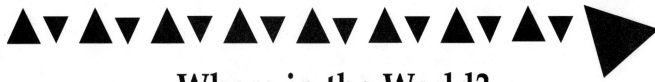

Where in the World?

Capitalization Rule: Capitalize proper nouns.
Capitalize specific places such as cities, states, and countries.

All proper nouns that name places are capitalized. The city and state in which you live are proper nouns and should be capitalized. This includes even the street on which you live.

Complete each sentence below to show the specific place you live. Capitalize each proper noun that names a place.

1. I live on _____.
(planet)

2. I live in _____.
(continent)

3. I live in _____.
(country)

4. I live in _____.
(state)

5. I live in _____.
(county)

6. I live in _____.
(city)

7. I live on _____.
(street)

Complete the sentence below with the information you wrote in the blanks above.

I live on _____ in _____
(planet)   (continent)

in _____ in _____
(country)   (state)

in _____ in _____
(county)   (city)

on _____.
(street)

Map It

Capitalization Rule: Capitalize proper nouns.
Capitalize specific places such as malls, buildings, and bridges.

Proper nouns that name places are always capitalized. The names of malls, buildings, bridges, parks, churches, schools, stores, and roads all need to be capitalized.

Practice capitalizing proper nouns that are places by labeling the map. Write a word from the word bank in the box next to each picture on the map.

Word Bank

Lamar Bridge	Ash Park	Hart Hospital
Oak School	Gainer Library	St. Peter Church
Town Bank	Main Post Office	

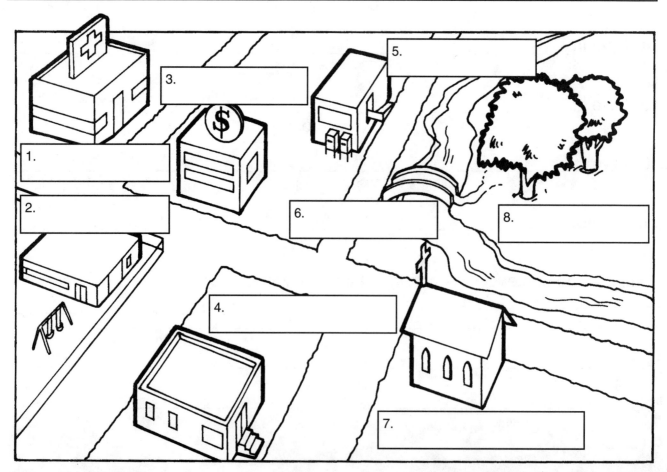

Brand Names

Capitalization Rule: Capitalize proper nouns.

Capitalize specific things such as brand names and the names of cars or games.

The names of things that are proper nouns are all capitalized. *The Mona Lisa*, Toyota, *Chutes and Ladders*, and Cheetos each name a specific thing. *The Mona Lisa* names a piece of art. *Toyota* is a company that makes cars. *Chutes and Ladders* is a game for children. *Cheetos* is a type of snack.

Write a proper noun for each of the things listed below. Capitalize each of the words you write.

1. tennis shoe _____

2. basketball team _____

3. cartoon_____

4. tissue _____

5. robot_____

6. toothpaste _____

7. video game _____

8. cookie _____

9. soap_____

10. soda_____

Write a sentence about one of the items that you listed above.

_____

_____

_____

Days of the Week

Capitalization Rule: Capitalize proper nouns.

Capitalize the names of specific things, such as the days of the week.

Monday, *Tuesday*, and *Wednesday* each name a specific day of the week. The days of the week are all capitalized.

Rewrite each of the days of the week, beginning each with a capital letter.

1. monday _____   5. friday _____

2. tuesday _____   6. saturday _____

3. wednesday _____   7. sunday _____

4. thursday _____

Write a sentence about something that you do on the following days of the week. Include the name of the day in your sentence. Be sure to capitalize the day of the week.

1. Monday   I have piano lessons on Monday.

2. Wednesday _____

3. Saturday _____

4. Sunday _____

Fill in the calendar below with the days of the week.

Sunday						

Answer the questions about the days of the week.

1. What is today? _____

2. What was yesterday? _____

3. What will tomorrow be? _____

4. What was the day before yesterday? _____

Months of the Year

Capitalization Rule: Capitalize proper nouns.
Capitalize specific things such as the months of the year.

Just as the days of the week are capitalized, the names of the months of the year are capitalized, too. All 12 months begin with a capital letter.

Practice the months of the year in order by singing them to the tune of "Mary Had a Little Lamb." Then, write the names of the months of the year on the lines below. Try writing them in order.

1. January _____

2. _____

3. _____

4. _____

5. _____

6. _____

7. _____

8. _____

9. _____

10. _____

11. _____

12. _____

1	2	3	4	5	6	7
8	9	10	11	12	13	14
15	16	17	18	19	20	21
22	23	24	25	26	27	28
29	30	31				

Write the month of your birthday on top of this calendar. Circle the date of your birthday. Then write a sentence about your birthday month.

_____

_____

Geography

Capitalization Rule: Capitalize proper nouns.
Capitalize specific geographic locations.

Geographic locations that have names are capitalized. The names of mountains, rivers, oceans, and waterfalls are proper nouns that name specific geographic locations.

Practice capitalizing geographic locations by choosing ones from the word bank to match the pictures below. Write the name of the location on the line.

Word Bank

Victoria Falls	Green Mountain	Catalina Island	Bick Forest
Wall Lake	Gear River	Pacific Ocean	Grand Bay

1. <u>Bick Forest</u>

5. _____

2. _____

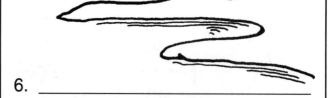

6. _____

3. _____

7. _____

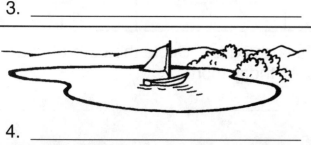

4. _____

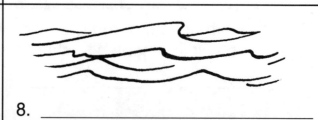

8. _____

Movies, Songs, and Plays

Capitalization Rule: Capitalize proper nouns.

Capitalize the names of movies, songs, television shows, and plays.

The names of specific movies, songs, television shows, and plays are all proper nouns and need to be capitalized. *Cinderella* names a specific movie. "Row, Row, Row Your Boat" names a song and *Mister Rogers' Neighborhood* names a television show. In each case, the proper noun was capitalized. Capitalize each word of the title if the title has more than one word. Do not capitalize words like *and, the, a*, and *or* unless one is the first word in the title.

Examples: *Snow White and the Seven Dwarfs, The Muppet Show*

Rewrite the following sentences, capitalizing the proper nouns that name movies, songs, television shows, or plays. The proper nouns are underlined for you.

1. Our class went to see <u>*the music man*</u>.

   <u>Our class went to see The Music Man.</u>

2. We sang a Thanksgiving song to the tune of "<u>frere jacques</u>."

   _____

3. My favorite cartoon show is <u>*looney toons*</u>.

   _____

4. <u>*the rescuers*</u> is now on video.

   _____

5. My sister kept singing "<u>mary had a little lamb</u>" over and over again.

   _____

What are your favorite things? On a separate piece of lined paper, write a list of your favorite things to answer the questions below. Capitalize your answers.

1. What is your favorite song?

2. What is your favorite movie?

3. What is your favorite television show?

4. What is your favorite play?

Names in the Media

> **Capitalization Rule:** Capitalize proper nouns.
>
> Capitalize media names or titles such as books, newspapers, and magazines.

The titles of books such as *The True Story of the Three Little Pigs* and *Peter Pan* name specific books and need to be capitalized. Just as with the titles of movies or television shows, capitalize all words in the title except words such as *and*, *for*, *of*, *or*, and *the* unless it is the first word of the title. Titles of newspapers and magazines also need to be capitalized.

Rewrite the names of these books, newspapers, and magazines, using capital letters.

Books

1. *alice in wonderland* _____
2. *charlotte's web* _____
3. *strega nona* _____
4. *if you give a mouse a cookie* _____

Newspapers

5. *new york times* _____
6. *the wall street journal* _____
7. *daily sun* _____
8. *the register* _____

Magazines

9. *cricket* _____
10. *time* _____
11. *highlights for children* _____
12. *ranger rick* _____

On the back of this paper, write a sentence about your favorite book. Be sure to capitalize the title of the book and tell why it is your favorite.

Religious and Political Holidays

Capitalization Rule: Capitalize proper nouns.
Capitalize the names of religious and political holidays.

The names of religious and political holidays are proper nouns that need to be *capitalized.* Read the sentences about the holidays. Write the name of the *italicized* holiday on the line next to each sentence. Remember to capitalize the name of the holiday.

1. Children play with dreidels during *hanukkah.* _____

2. There are seven symbols of *kwanzaa.* _____

3. The United States celebrates its independence on the *fourth of july.*

   _____

4. *memorial day* is a time to remember loved ones who died for our country.

   _____

5. Symbols of *st. patrick's day* are leprechauns and shamrocks.

   _____

6. On *martin luther king, jr. day,* we remember the things Martin Luther King, Jr. did for civil rights. _____

7. On *christmas,* Santa brings presents to good boys and girls.

   _____

8. A traditional *thanksgiving day* dinner is turkey, cranberries, and mashed potatoes. _____

9. A bunny will leave you a basket of eggs if you celebrate *easter.*

   _____

10. On *presidents' day,* we celebrate the birthdays of Washington and Lincoln.

    _____

Calendar Holidays

Capitalization Rule: Capitalize proper nouns.
Capitalize the names of holidays.

There are many other holidays that are not religious or political. The names of these holidays are capitalized, too. Sandwich Day, Valentine's Day, and Halloween are examples of holidays that need to be capitalized too.

Write the name of the holiday under each picture that represents the holiday. Choose words from the word bank.

Word Bank

New Year's Eve/Day   Valentine's Day   Father's Day

Groundhog Day   April Fool's Day   Halloween

Mother's Day   Earth Day   Columbus Day

1. _____

2. _____

3. _____

4. _____

5. _____

6. _____

7. _____

8. _____

9. _____

Assessment: Proper Nouns

Option 1

Rewrite the words on the lines below. If the word needs to be capitalized, capitalize it when you write it. If the word does not need to be capitalized, copy it below.

1. house _____

2. mary _____

3. tuesday _____

4. pet _____

5. december _____

6. yellow _____

7. *sesame street* _____

8. paper _____

9. boy _____

10. chicago _____

11. *cinderella* _____

12. school _____

13. *the new york times* _____

14. thanskgiving day _____

Write a sentence about one of the proper nouns listed above.

_____

_____

_____

Assessment: Proper Nouns *(cont.)*

Option 2

Rewrite the following sentences on the lines below. Capitalize words that need capitalization. See if you can find all 22 words. On the back of this paper, write a short story about your favorite month of the year.

My Favorite Time of Year

My favorite month of the year is november. The fourth thursday in november is thanksgiving day. It is a time for friends and family to get together and celebrate all of the things for which we are thankful. On thanksgiving, my family travels to boston, massachusetts, to be with my grandma. All of the joneses gather for a big meal. Uncle tim and aunt sarah come with their children, mary, allen, and patrick. We watch the macy's thanksgiving day parade on television. My favorite balloons are barney and garfield. My grandma prepares a wonderful meal of turkey, mashed potatoes, and, of course, pumpkin pie. After dinner, we watch football on television. It is nice to be with family on thanksgiving. We have a fun time.

_____

_____

_____

_____

_____

_____

_____

_____

Very Important People

| **Capitalization Rule:** Capitalize proper nouns. |
| Capitalize the title given to a person. |

A title should always be capitalized if a person's name follows the title. General George Washington and Queen Victoria are two examples of titles that need to be capitalized. Often a title is followed by a person's name. Both the title and the name need to be capitalized. Practice capitalizing the titles and names listed below by rewriting the titles and names on the lines.

1. captain hook

   Captain Hook _____

2. doctor doolittle

   _____

3. king henry

   _____

4. president lincoln

   _____

5. judge wilson

   _____

6. saint patrick

   _____

In the sentences below, circle each title and name.

7. I am going to Doctor Swan's for a checkup.

8. President Washington was the first president of the United States.

9. General Patton led the troops.

10. The next leader of England will be Prince Charles.

11. Private May was in charge of the helicopter.

12. Judge Wills dismissed the case.

Titles of People

Capitalization Rule: Capitalize proper nouns.
Capitalize the title given to a person.

A title needs to be capitalized if the person's name follows the title.

Practice capitalizing the titles and names by writing a complete sentence about each title. Be sure to capitalize the title as well as the name that follows.

1. Doctor Mays   _____

                                _____

2. Mister Calvin   _____

                                 _____

3. Princess Anne   _____

                                 _____

4. Coach Douglas   _____

                                 _____

5. Queen Mary   _____

                                 _____

Think of four more people who have titles. Write their names on the lines below.

1. _____   3. _____

2. _____   4. _____

Shortened Words

Capitalization Rule: Capitalize abbreviations for proper nouns.

An abbreviation is a short way to write another word. For example, the abbreviation for "Doctor" is "Dr." Instead of writing "Doctor Tanner," you could write "Dr. Tanner." An abbreviation is often the first few letters of the word or the initials of a group of words. An abbreviation that stands for a proper noun is always capitalized.

Rewrite the following abbreviations on the lines next to them. Notice where the periods are placed in each abbreviation. When you rewrite the abbreviation, be sure to capitalize it.

Draw a line from each of the abbreviations to the word or words it replaces.

1. mar. _Mar._____

2. gen. _____

3. h.r.h. _____

4. d.c. _____

5. tues. _____

6. b.a. _____

7. capt. _____

8. f.b.i. _____

Her Royal Highness Queen Elizabeth

Captain Hook

Bachelor of Arts

Tuesday

Federal Bureau of Investigation

General Lee

March

District of Columbia

Calendar Terms

> **Capitalization Rule:** Capitalize abbreviations for proper nouns.

Some of the most common abbreviations are the months of the year and the days of the week. Remember that the names of the months and days are capitalized because they are proper nouns. The abbreviations for the months and days are capitalized, too.

Write the correct abbreviation for each word on the line next to the word. Use the abbreviation bank to help you write the words correctly.

Abbreviation Bank				
Jan.	Aug.	Feb.	Thurs.	Sat.
Sept.	Nov.	Sun.	Wed.	Mon.

1. January _____
2. February _____
3. August _____
4. September_____
5. November _____

6. Monday _____
7. Wednesday _____
8. Thursday _____
9. Saturday _____
10. Sunday _____

Draw a line from each word to its abbreviation..

11. Feb.   Friday

12. Apr.   April

13. Dec.   December

14. Tues.   February

15. Fri.   Tuesday

Label the States

Capitalization Rule: Capitalize abbreviations for proper nouns.

Another common use for abbreviations is for geographic locations such as states. The name of the state is a proper noun and must be capitalized. The abbreviation must also be capitalized.

Below are two maps that show some states. On the first map, the name of each state is indicated. Label the blank map with the correct abbreviation for each state. The names of the states and their abbreviations are in the Abbreviation Bank below.

Abbreviation Bank

Arizona	AZ	Montana	MT	Utah	UT
California	CA	Nevada	NV	Washington	WA
Colorado	CO	New Mexico	NM	Wyoming	WY
Idaho	ID	Oregon	OR		

Titles and Abbreviations Assessment

Listed below are titles that can be given to a person. Write a sentence using the title with the name of a person.

1. doctor _____

_____

2. senator _____

_____

3. president _____

_____

4. king _____

_____

Listed below are abbreviations. Rewrite the abbreviation on the line next to each one. If the abbreviation needs to be capitalized, capitalize it when you recopy it.

5. ny _____   10. f.b.i _____

6. ia _____   11. wed. _____

7. mon. _____   12. h.r.h. _____

8. mar._____   13. ca _____

9. dec._____   14. jan. _____

Writing a Letter

Capitalization Rules: Capitalize the first word of a greeting and closing in a letter.

Capitalize proper nouns.

There are many places you need to capitalize words in a letter. The greeting and closing of a letter each begin with a capital letter. The proper nouns that are in a letter need to be capitalized, too. Notice all of the places that words are capitalized in the letter below.

November 20, 1999 → date

greeting →
person's name → Dear Isabelle,

body → { I am writing to invite you to my birthday party. The party will be on Tuesday, December 7, 1999. It will begin at 2 P.M. I hope you will be able to come.

Love, ← closing
Martha

P.S. We will be having chocolate cake.

Practice capitalizing the following greetings and closings by writing each on the line next to it. The first word of each heading and closing is the only word that is capitalized.

1. yours truly, _____

2. love, _____

3. best wishes, _____

4. sincerely yours, _____

5. with love, _____

6. sincerely, _____

7. dear _____

8. respectfully, _____

Extension: Pretend you are Isabelle and write to Martha to let her know whether or not you will be coming to the birthday party. Write your letter on the back of this paper.

Thanks for the Gift

Capitalization Rules: Capitalize the first word of a greeting and closing in a letter.

Capitalize abbreviations for proper nouns.

Practice capitalizing the greeting, closing, and proper nouns by writing a letter to your friend to thank him or her for the birthday gift he or she gave you. Use the template below to help you write your letter.

```
                                                    _____
                                                             (date)

_____,
        (greeting)
      ┌  _____
      │  _____
      │  _____
      │  _____
 body │  _____
      │  _____
      │  _____
      └  _____

                                         _____
                                                 (closing)

                                         _____
                                                (signature)
```

Extension: Research the format of a business letter. Practice writing a business letter. What other words do you have to capitalize in a business letter?

Unit Assessment

Option 1

During your life you will have to fill out many forms. When you fill out a form, there are many words that you will need to capitalize. Knowing which word to capitalize is important. Show what you know about capitalization by filling out the Student Information Card below. Be sure to capitalize words that need to begin with a capital letter.

Student Information Card

First Name	Middle Name	Last Name

Age	Birthday	

Street Address		

City	State	Zip code

Grade Level

What is the title of your favorite television show?

What is the title of your favorite book?

Write two sentences about your favorite subjects in school.
_____ _____ _____

Unit Assessment *(cont.)*

Option 2

Show what you have learned about capitalization by copying the following paragraph. Capitalize any words that need a capital letter when you rewrite it.

i have a dream

dr. martin luther king, jr. is a famous person from american history. through boycotts and protests, king worked for equal rights for black citizens of the united states. he did not think that blacks should have to sit at the back of the bus. in 1955 he helped organize a boycott of the busses in montgomery, alabama. in august 1963, he led a large group in a march on washington. the people gathered in washington, d.c., to support a civil rights bill. as they gathered around the lincoln memorial, martin luther king, jr. gave his most famous speech, known as the "i have a dream" speech. to this day, martin luther king, jr. is known for his peaceful protests, support for civil rights, and his famous speech.

_____

_____

_____

_____

_____

_____

_____

_____

42

Self–Assessment

Respond to these statements to indicate what you have learned about capitalization.

1. The easiest thing for me to remember to capitalize is . . .

   _____

2. My way of remembering to capitalize is to . . .

   _____

3. I still have trouble remembering to capitalize . . .

   _____

4. When I have trouble remembering what to capitalize, I . . .

   _____

5. I'm not sure I understand how or why to capitalize . . .

   _____

6. I think I could teach someone else how to capitalize . . .

   _____

7. I would be a good teacher because . . .

   _____

Capitalization Reference Page

Use capital letters for all of the following:

- **The pronoun I**

  Yesterday I went to the movies.

- **The first word of every sentence.**

  It is going to rain today.

- **Proper Nouns**

  Names of People

  Abraham Lincoln

  Names of Places

  Central Park, Iowa, Canada

  Names of Things

  Toyota, Coca Cola

  Days of the Week

  Monday, Friday

  Months of the Year

  January, February

  Movies, Songs, Plays

  Annie, "Frere Jacques"

  Geographic Locations

  Mount Hood, Ohio River

  Books, Newspapers, Magazines, TV Shows

  Stega Nona, Sesame Street, Time

Religious and Political Holidays and Calendar Holidays

Thanksgiving, Easter, Labor Day

Titles followed by proper nouns

Queen Mary, Mister Calvin

Abbreviations for proper nouns

Dr., IA, Wed., Mar.

The greeting and closing in a letter

Dear Sirs, Sincerely, Best wishes,

- **Abbreviations for Titles**

Assistant—Asst.	Mister—Mr.
Attorney—Atty.	President—Pres.
Captain—Capt.	Principal—Princ.
Colonel—Col.	Reverend—Rev.
Doctor—Dr.	Sergeant—Sgt.
General—Gen.	Saint—St.

His (Her)
Royal Highness H.R.H.

State Abbreviations

Alabama	AL	Indiana	IN	Nebraska	NE	South Carolina	SC
Alaska	AK	Iowa	IA	Nevada	NV	South Dakota	SD
Arizona	AZ	Kansas	KS	New Hampshire	NH	Tennessee	TN
Arkansas	AR	Kentucky	KY	New Jersey	NJ	Texas	TX
California	CA	Louisiana	LA	New Mexico	NM	Utah	UT
Colorado	CO	Maine	ME	New York	NY	Vermont	VT
Connecticut	CT	Maryland	MD	North Carolina	NC	Virginia	VA
Delaware	DE	Massachusetts	MA	North Dakota	ND	Washington	WA
Florida	FL	Michigan	MI	Ohio	OH	West Virginia	WV
Georgia	GA	Minnesota	MN	Oklahoma	OK	Wisconsin	WI
Hawaii	HI	Mississippi	MS	Oregon	OR	Wyoming	WY
Idaho	ID	Missouri	MO	Pennsylvania	PA		
Illinois	IL	Montana	MT	Rhode Island	RI		

Certificate and Reference Posters

Hippo Hurray!
I know how to capitalize!

Name

_____   _____
Date   Teacher's Signature

Capitalizing in a Sentence

The first word of every sentence begins with a capital letter. It shows the reader that a new sentence has started.

Every sentence begins with a capital letter.

Reference Poster

The word *I* takes the place of your name. You always begin your name with a capital letter. The word *I* is always capitalized too. You can remember this saying: *When the **I** stands alone, it stands tall.*

The word I is always capitalized.

Capitalizing in a Sentence

Words that are proper nouns name specific persons, places, and things. Always capitalize these names.

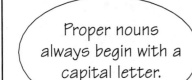

Proper nouns always begin with a capital letter.

Proper nouns name people, states, days, months, movies, holidays, and much, much more.

Answer Key

Page 4

A B C D E F G H I J K L M
N O P Q R S T U V W X Y Z

Page 5

1. F
2. S
3. U
4. K
5. F, L
6. O, V
7. H, L
8. W, Z
9. S, U, W
10. K, L, N, P, Q, S

Page 6

Bunny
Parrot

Page 7

All answers: I

Page 8

1. I like ice cream.
2. I have a pet lizard.
3. I am going to the park after school.
4. I helped my mom plant a garden.
5. On Sunday, I am going to my grandma's house.
6. I don't like spinach.
7. On Saturday, I am going to a birthday party.
8. I have a lot of homework today.
9. If I do my chores, I get an allowance.
10. I learned to ride a bike when I was six.

Page 10

Answers will vary but should begin as the following:

1. I am …
2. I am …
3. I was born …
4. I have …
5. I have …
6. I have …
7. I am in …
8. I go to …

Page 11

1. My
2. Can
3. Are
4. I
5. We
6. She
7. There

Page 12

1. Today is my birthday.
2. My sister walked to the store with me.
3. We are going to play handball at recess.
4. Can you come to the park with us?
5. Our class has a pet lizard.
6. Juan ate a sandwich for lunch.
7. The rabbit likes to eat carrots.
8. My blue crayon is missing.
9. Dad is going to take us to the park this weekend.
10. I am going to the library after school.

Page 14

Wording may vary. Check that the first word of each sentence begins with a capital letter.

1. The three bears went for a walk.
2. Goldilocks came into the bears' house.
3. Goldilocks ate all of Baby Bear's porridge.
4. Goldilocks sat on the chairs.
5. Mama Bear's bed was too soft.
6. Goldilocks ran out of the house.

Page 15

1. My brother plays soccer.
2. Dad gave me a doll.
3. I have to take out the trash.
4. We rode our bikes.
5. Mom and I went to the store.
6. May I use your pencil?
7. I like to read books about bugs.
8. My favorite food is pizza.

Page 16

After school today, I went to my friend Sam's house. We played soccer. Sam is good at scoring goals. I am good at passing the ball. After we played soccer, we went in the house. Mrs. Matthews had cookies for us to eat. We had milk too. Milk is good with cookies. When we were done eating, we watched television. It started to get late, so I went home.

Page 17

1. Tuesday
2. December
3. Illinois
4. Mississippi River
5. Anne
6. Dr. Andrews
7. *The Little Engine That Could*
8. Thanksgiving Day
9. Washington, D.C.
10. *Ranger Rick*

Page 19

1. Roger Taper
2. Silvia Mantos
3. Clarissa Choi
4. Tammy Lynn Witter
5. Victor Jason Lee

Page 21

1. Hart Hospital
2. Oak School
3. Town Bank
4. Gainer Library
5. Main Post Office
6. Lamar Bridge
7. St. Peter Church
8. Ash Park

Page 24

1. Monday
2. Tuesday
3. Wednesday
4. Thursday
5. Friday
6. Saturday
7. Sunday

Page 25

1. January
2. February
3. March
4. April
5. May
6. June
7. July
8. August
9. September
10. October
11. November
12. December

Page 26

1. Bick Forest
2. Gear River
3. Victoria Falls
4. Wall Lake
5. Green Mountain
6. Grand Bay
7. Catalina Island
8. Pacific Ocean

Page 27

1. Our class went to see *The Music Man*.
2. We sang a Thanksgiving song to the tune of "Frere Jacques."
3. My favorite cartoon show is *Looney Toons*.

Answer Key (cont.)

4. *The Rescuers* is now on video.
5. My sister kept singing "Mary Had a Little Lamb" over and over again.

Page 28
1. *Alice in Wonderland*
2. *Charlotte's Web*
3. *Strega Nona*
4. *If You Give a Mouse a Cookie*
5. *New York Times*
6. *The Wall Street Journal*
7. *Daily Sun*
8. *The Register*
9. *Cricket*
10. *Time*
11. *Highlights for Children*
12. *Ranger Rick*

Page 29
1. Hanukkah
2. Kwanzaa
3. Fourth of July
4. Memorial Day
5. St. Patrick's Day
6. Martin Luther King, Jr. Day
7. Christmas
8. Thanksgiving Day
9. Easter
10. Presidents' Day

Page 30
1. New Year's Eve/Day
2. Valentine's Day
3. Father's Day
4. Groundhog Day
5. April Fool's Day
6. Halloween
7. Mother's Day
8. Earth Day
9. Columbus Day

Page 31
1. house
2. Mary
3. Tuesday
4. pet
5. December

6. yellow
7. *Sesame Street*
8. paper
9. boy
10. Chicago
11. *Cinderella*
12. school
13. *The New York Times*
14. Thanksgiving Day

Page 32
My favorite month of the year is November. The fourth Thursday in November is Thanksgiving Day. It is a time for friends and family to get together and celebrate all of the things for which we are thankful. On Thanksgiving, my family travels to Boston, Massachusetts, to be with my grandma. All of the Joneses gather for a big meal. Uncle Tim and Aunt Sarah come with their children, Mary, Allen, and Patrick. We watch the Macy's Thanksgiving Day Parade on television. My favorite balloons are Barney and Garfield. My grandma prepares a wonderful meal of turkey, mashed potatoes, and, of course, pumpkin pie. After dinner, we watch football on television. It is nice to be with family on Thanksgiving. We have a fun time.

Page 33
1. Captain Hook
2. Doctor Doolittle
3. King Henry
4. President Lincoln
5. Judge Wilson
6. Saint Patrick
7. Doctor Swan's
8. President Washington
9. General Patton
10. Prince Charles
11. Private May
12. Judge Wills

Page 35
1. Mar.—March
2. Gen.—General
3. H.R.H.—Her Royal Highness
4. D.C.—District of Columbia
5. Tues.—Tuesday
6. B.A.—Bachelor of Arts
7. Capt.—Captain
8. F.B.I.—Federal Bureau of Investigation

Page 36
1. Jan.
2. Feb.
3. Aug.
4. Sept.
5. Nov.
6. Mon.
7. Wed.
8. Thurs.
9. Sat.
10. Sun.
11. Feb.—February
12. Apr.—April
13. Dec.—December
14. Tues.—Tuesday
15. Fri.—Friday

Page 37

Page 38
1–4. Answers will vary.
5. NY
6. IA
7. Mon.
8. Mar.

9. Dec.
10. F.B.I.
11. Wed.
12. H.R.H.
13. CA
14. Jan.

Page 39
1. Yours truly,
2. Love,
3. Best wishes,
4. Sincerely yours,
5. With love,
6. Sincerely,
7. Dear
8. Respectfully,

Page 42
I Have a Dream

Dr. Martin Luther King, Jr. is a famous person from American history. Through boycotts and protests, King worked for equal rights for black citizens of the United States. He did not think that blacks should have to sit at the back of the bus. In 1955 he helped organize a boycott of the busses in Montgomery, Alabama. In August 1963, he led a large group in a march on Washington. the people gathered in Washington, D.C., to support a civil rights bill. As they gathered around the Lincoln Memorial, Martin Luther King, Jr. gave his most famous speech, known as the "I Have a Dream" speech. To this day, Martin Luther King, Jr. is known for his peaceful protests, support for civil rights, and his famous speech.